JOELLYN DUESBERRY

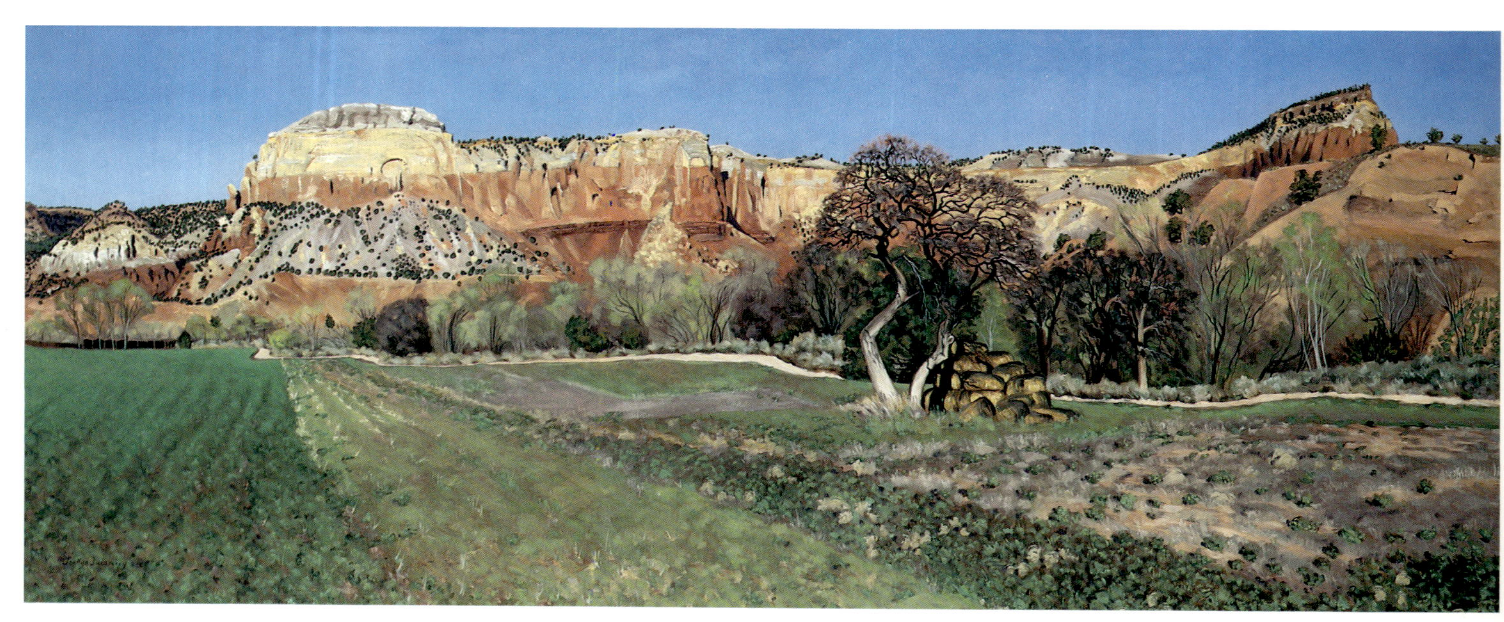

JOELLYN DUESBERRY

July 25 – August 9, 1986

GERALD PETERS GALLERY

SANTA FE, NEW MEXICO

COVER:
Red Hills and Ruth's Rock, January, 1986.
Oil on linen, 28 x 22 in. Initialed lower right.

FRONTISPIECE:
1   *Kitchen Mesa and Alfalfa Field, Ghost Ranch*, April, 1986.
Oil on canvas, 30 x 72 in. Signed lower left.

The Gerald Peters Gallery wishes to thank Julie Schimmel
for her introductory essay.
Exhibition and catalogue coordinated by Gayle Maxon with
the assistance of Quincie Hopkins.

© Copyright 1986 The Peters Corporation

LIBRARY OF CONGRESS CATALOG CARD: 86–60902
ISBN: 0–935037–10–1

PHOTOGRAPHY: Monica McCoy and Warren Hanford
DESIGN: Eleanor Caponigro
PRINTING: Columbine Printing Company, Taos
BINDING: Roswell Book Binding, Phoenix

Artist's Statement

It seems that all I know of art history—the Dutch beginnings in landscape, the Italian, the Hudson River school, the Taos school, etc.—is totally irrelevant to the arid moonscape I find myself attracted to here. There is no precedent for me, no elder whispering directives at my shoulder, no grand old master encouraging me or stunning me mute. There is no help anywhere. And so, something like absolute freedom makes for joy in all the awkwardness of the new song—I know no words, so I hum and make it all up as I go along. Every now and then my hand will devise some new gesture to render the fuzz and prickle of winter chamisa or sage or the gum-drop precision of piñon against powdery dryness, so that the virgin territory will feel a bit more familiar, domesticated. But for the most part, I am groping to capture an arid oddness that is non-East Coast, non-European in those cumulative traditions of the beautiful in landscape.

I have been dazzled by the crowded and textured desert floor and have begun to render foreground in detail as never before. It's harder than ever to stay in the comfort of middle and background, "the parts of the canvas in which the painter's mark best approximates what we would see were we actually looking at nature," because out here all sense of scale is unfamiliar, self-contradicting. The vastness is relentless, and yet the speed of curves in hills is genuine. An intimacy is implied by small piñon dots, and yet as they clump at hillcrests they imply a panorama and a distance out of human reach. One other paradox about the desert which excites me the most of all is its seasonless busy-ness. At all times of year the big arid emptiness is in fact a *horror vacuii* of insistent detail, inviting an over-all painting approach, with the cue taken from the foreground. Even in winter, odd shrubs and cacti rattle their dried flowers and seeds in ornamental patterns, and the skeletons of cottonwood and chamisa are a woolly softness against the black, thorny dead shrub.

JOELLYN DUESBERRY
From letter, April 7, 1986, to Blair T. Birmelin, writer, *Art in America*

The Art of Joellyn Duesberry

Joellyn Duesberry became a painter at age ten, when the sunset light of Virginia Beach struck her new red tennis shoes. Although just a child, the dazzle of peach sand, purple shadows, and red shoes led her to put picture to paper with oil paints given to her by her grandmother. So began a career shaped by high intelligence, intense enthusiasms, and unwavering determination.

Born in 1944 in Richmond, Virginia, Duesberry's family was ambitious for her. She was raised as an accomplished woman of southern graces, but her drive to paint soon took over her genteel upbringing. While in preparatory school, she discovered that the artist of a scene of red hills on a postcard was not "George" O'Keeffe, as it was mistakenly printed, but "Georgia." Women artists existed and she intended to be among them.

Duesberry's training took serious direction when she entered Mary Washington College of the University of Virginia. Here, Dorothy Van Winckel, a pastellist, encouraged her talent, and, here, she found a place among other maverick women with similar ambitions to paint. Transferring to Smith College for her junior year, Duesberry fought for studio space, where she began to absorb all she could of western painting traditions beginning with the early Renaissance. Convinced that she was too impressionable, she worked to absorb and then exorcise the work of artists who might too readily sway her art in future years.

Smith College awarded Duesberry a Woodrow Wilson fellowship that paid her way to the prestigious Institute of Fine Arts, a graduate department in art history at New York University. The degree gave her the background she needed to become an appraiser, specializing in seventeenth-century Dutch and Flemish paintings as well as in Impressionism. This assured a source of income from the late sixties until the early eighties, while she devoted the majority of her time to her true passion—painting.

Swayed by art world enthusiasms for abstract art in the 1960s, her first work was non-objective. However, her sensitivity to nature soon showed through and the abstracted patterns of tree roots, lichen patterns on rocks, or waterfalls formed the basis of her imagery. She next went through a ten-year period in which urban views preoccupied her, but, after a trek to Peru where she was dazzled by the Andes, she re-discovered landscape.

Duesberry's current landscapes reflect the enormous pleasure she takes in the land of New Mexico, which she first painted in February, 1985. The specific quality of individual places are important to her as her titles suggest: *Taos at Noon from the Gorge* or *Morning, Painted Desert at Abiquiu* (plates 9 and 18). She likes to feel that balmy, damp, or sunny weather finds its way into her painting, and, indeed, it does. Winter cold is palpable in *Chatfield Reservoir, Chamisa and Snow*; the humid heat of an August day can be felt in *Red Hills, Abiquiu* (plates 8 and 10).

The scenes that choose her to paint them (as she describes it) are usually ones in which some special quirk of man or nature exists. In *High Desert Farm at Ghost Ranch* (plate 2), the angled pattern of leafless tree branches and irregularly stacked bales of hay catch the artist's eye, and, she, in turn, passes the image through her unique sense of form and holds it up for us to see. The scattered pattern of rooftops in *Tin Roofs, Chimayo*, the jerry-built barbed-wire gate in *Dixon's Orchard, La Cañada*, or the black-and-white striped cattleguard in *Approaching Abiquiu*—these are the eye-catching arabesque and geometric patterns that draw the artist to a painting site (plates 14, 7, and 15). Similarly, the sunken, circular watering hole in *Cliffs from Chimney to Ruth's Rock* is the centrifugal center of shapes and planes that revolve around it (plate 5).

Her stance in the landscape is dictated by the scene before her, yet her instinct is drawn to the challenge of delicate balances. In *Melting Pond Ice at Abiquiu* (plate 17) she captures both the quality of solid and liquid water, one a blurred surface which only murkily reflects the surroundings, the other a sparkling plane that mirrors flanking hills. Boldly slicing the pond down the middle, she works the curved edge of the bank against the strong vertical of the painting and the undulating curves of rock formations.

Both the nearby and faraway are subjects of Duesberry's art. In *Red Hills and Ruth's Rock*, the artist fills the canvas space with the striated sandstone cliffs and eroded hills of Abiquiu (plate 12). We are in close company with these massive shapes, witness to pastel shades of lavender and yellow, saturated hues of mauve and burnt sienna, and contrasts of hard and soft-edged shapes. *Morning, Painted Desert at Abiquiu* is the same scene, but the artist has stepped back from the subject, dwelling on foreground clumps of green desert shrubbery and a ribbon dirt road that winds back into the hills (plate 18).

In yet other scenes, Duesberry grapples with the strange phenomenon of many New Mexico vistas which leap from near to far. This is especially true of her landscapes of Taos, in which the eye is led swiftly across barely differentiated foreground spaces to distant mountains. Only the brilliant yellow of desert growth in *Taos at Noon from the Gorge* breaks the eye's surge toward the far mountain range (plate 9).

Once present in a room of Duesberry paintings, it is impossible to drive through New Mexico without feeling that you are passing through a Duesberry scene. It is not simply her ability to pick out features that identify a geographic area or capture the spirit of place. It is Duesberry's ability to mix paints that recreate the extraordinary hues that typify New Mexican landscape. She is able to capture the dusky plum of distant mountains, the lime greens of desert grass, the mauves of desert hills, and the deep green of New Mexico's gumdrop vegetation. The variation she brings to the color blue alone suggests the maturity of a skill twenty years in the making. The blues in scenes painted of Chatfield Reservoir, near Denver, Colorado, range from the clear, light blues of sky in *Chatfield Reservoir, Chamisa and Snow* to the murky, deep blue of *Ice Fishing Huts at Chatfield* (plates 8 and 16).

Beyond subject, Duesberry's intense fascination with the craft of her art shows. She weaves a surface skin of unlimited sensations, yet each form has independent life of its own. While she sometimes paints on canvas, she frequently paints on masonite or wood panel. These surfaces are, as she phrases it, a slippery free-for-all and challenge her ability to control paint application. Perhaps it is in composition that Duesberry most challenges herself, however. A road enters from the lower left corner and shears steeply off to the right in *Orchard and the Road to La Cañada Ruin* (plate 7). The eye jumps to this pathway placed off-center in the canvas, yet its demanding presence is miraculously balanced by the disarray of fence posts in the immediate foreground and in the rhythm of gullies, ditches, and embankments that fan out to the left from the road.

Orchards at Velarde (plate 13) is another painting of compositional daring. Viewed from above, the scene stretches out in front of us, the eye moving from cultivated fields to uncultivated nature. One is careful geometry of plowed fields and orchards; the other irregular alternations of bare earth and desert growth. Within the square format, there is no single focal point, yet the eye explores path and gully without fatigue, the path of discovery relieved occasionally by the geometrical form of house or outbuilding.

Chimayo Farm along Route 76 (plate 11) is a study in motion, like the melody line in an upbeat tune. We plunge down into the foreground, spinning around the curving arroyo in the foreground, jumping over low hills into the middle ground, and then skipping from one plane to another in the distant mountains. The sensation is pleasant and playful.

Increasingly, Duesberry's pictures grow in size, so that side by side with 12 × 12 inch panels are paintings of considerably greater dimensions. One of the most ambitious of these is *Arroyo del Oso and Rancho Chonito Orchards, Chimayo* (plate 6). Measuring 26 × 72 inches, it is a panoramic view with the challenges that are by now familiar. An arroyo slashes in from the left, dividing the canvas unevenly. There are quirky objects that catch the eye, a contrast between cultivated and uncultivated lands, and a whimsical juxtaposition of modernistic architecture on the right and its country surroundings.

Duesberry's landscapes are tranquil in impact, yet vibrant in nuance. The wild color and sharp silhouettes that elate her are artfully tamed in scenes of delicate balance. Here in the Southwest, she has found once again that first hurtful light she discovered as a child at Virginia Beach. Now, as then, intense sensation leads to creation of images, which, in their New Mexican form, she describes as a "song for which I don't know the words, so I hum."

JULIE SCHIMMEL

2   *High Desert Farm at Ghost Ranch*, January, 1986.
Oil on linen, 26 × 72 in.
Signed lower right.

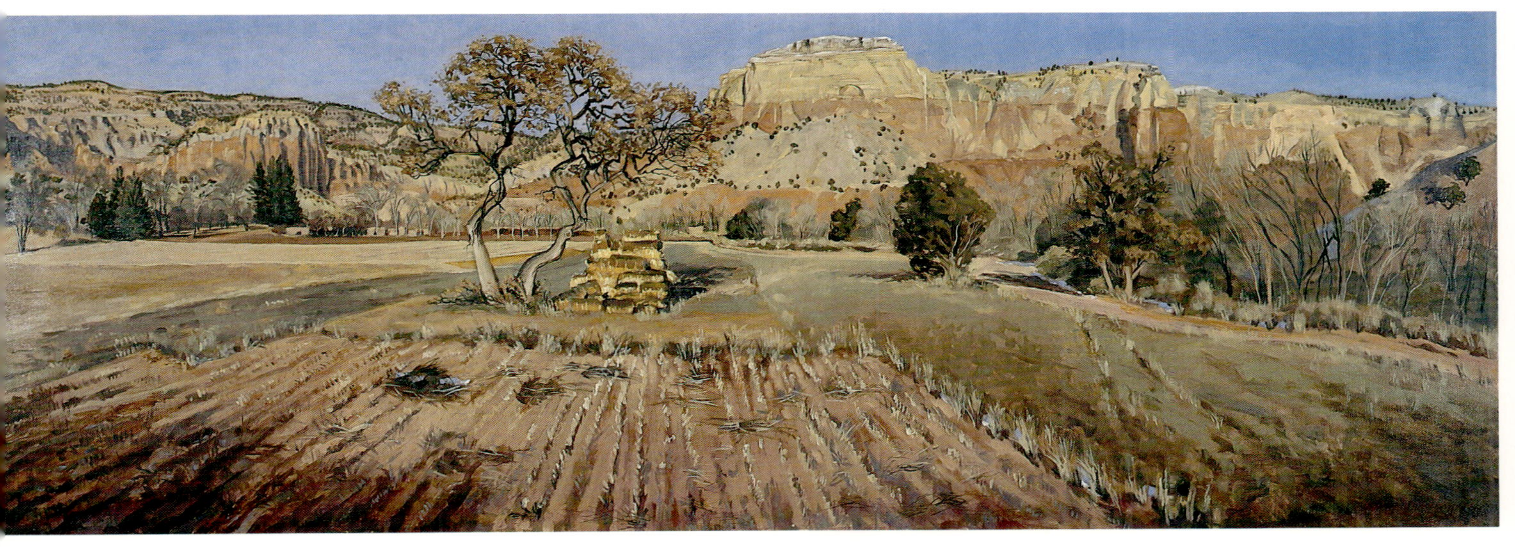

3   *Dixon's Orchard in Bloom (from La Cañada Ruin)*, April, 1986.
Oil on canvas, 28 × 48 in.
Initialed lower left.

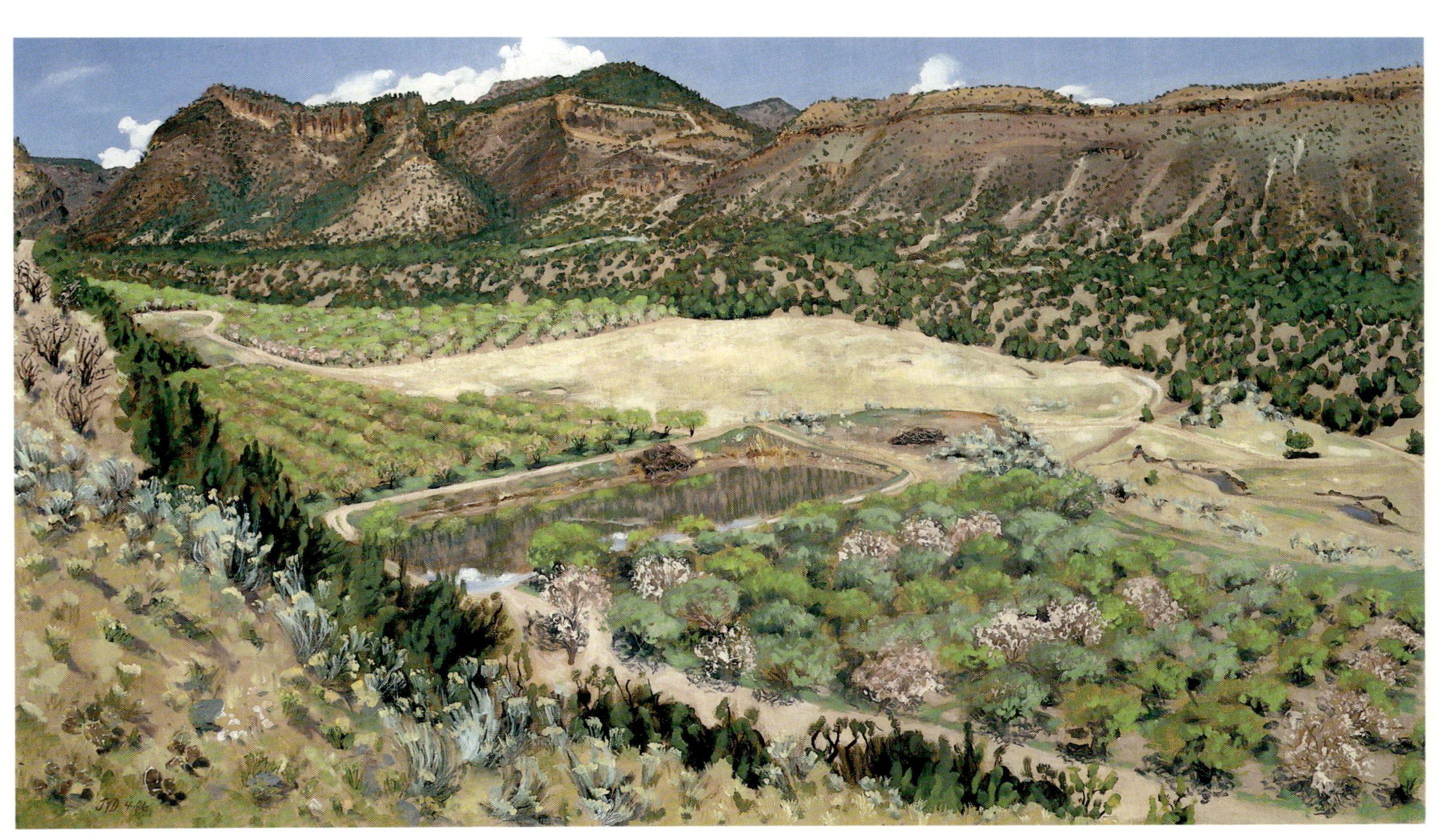

4   *Dixon's Orchard and Tetilla Peak, Evening,* March–April, 1986.
     Oil on canvas, 16 × 32 in.
     Initialed lower right.

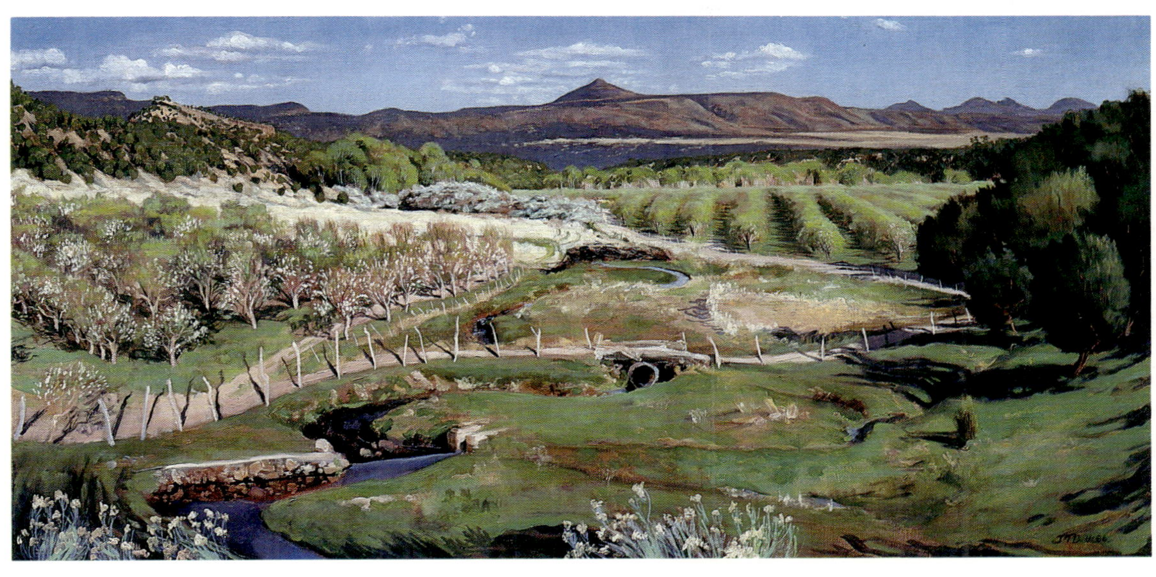

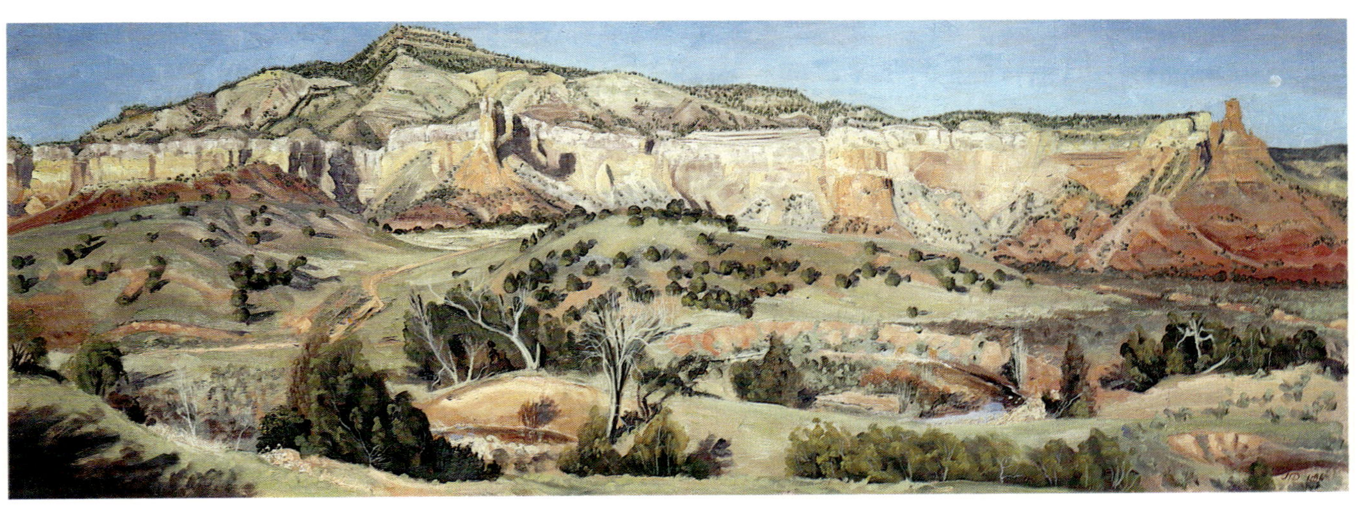

6   *Arroyo del Oso and Rancho Chonito Orchards, Chimayo*, February, 1986.
Oil on linen, 26 × 72 in.
Signed lower left.

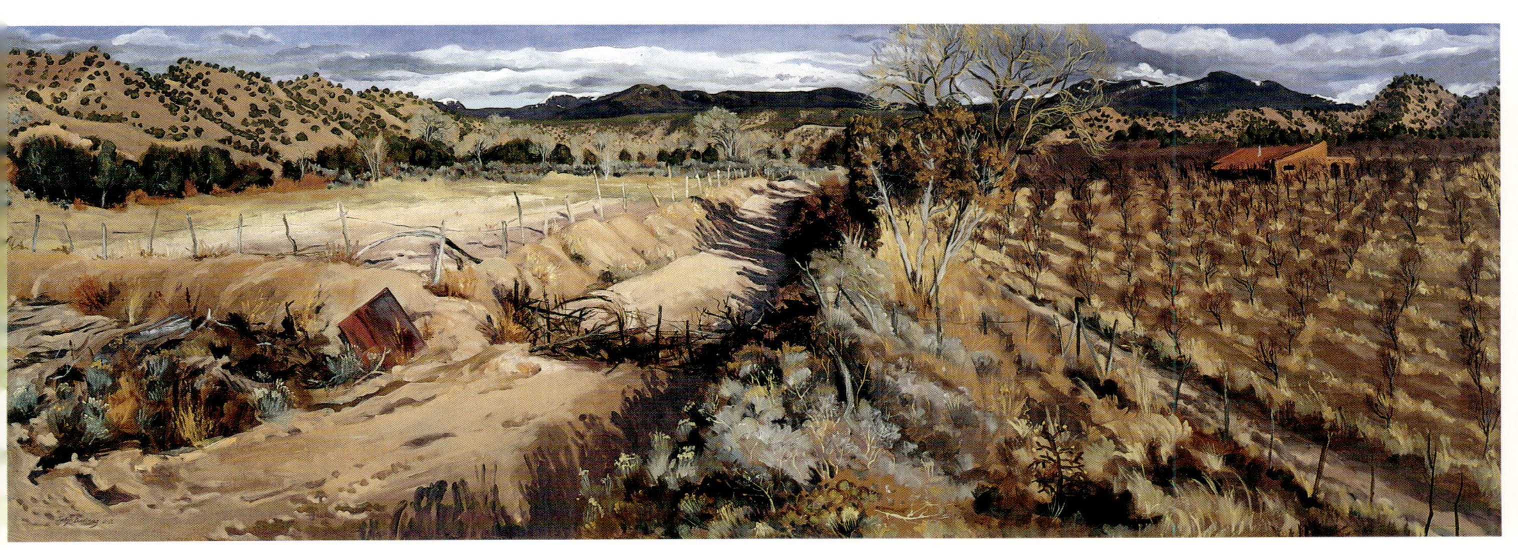

7   *Dixon's Orchard, La Cañada*, late March, 1986.
     Oil on linen, 24 × 36 in.
     Initialed lower left.

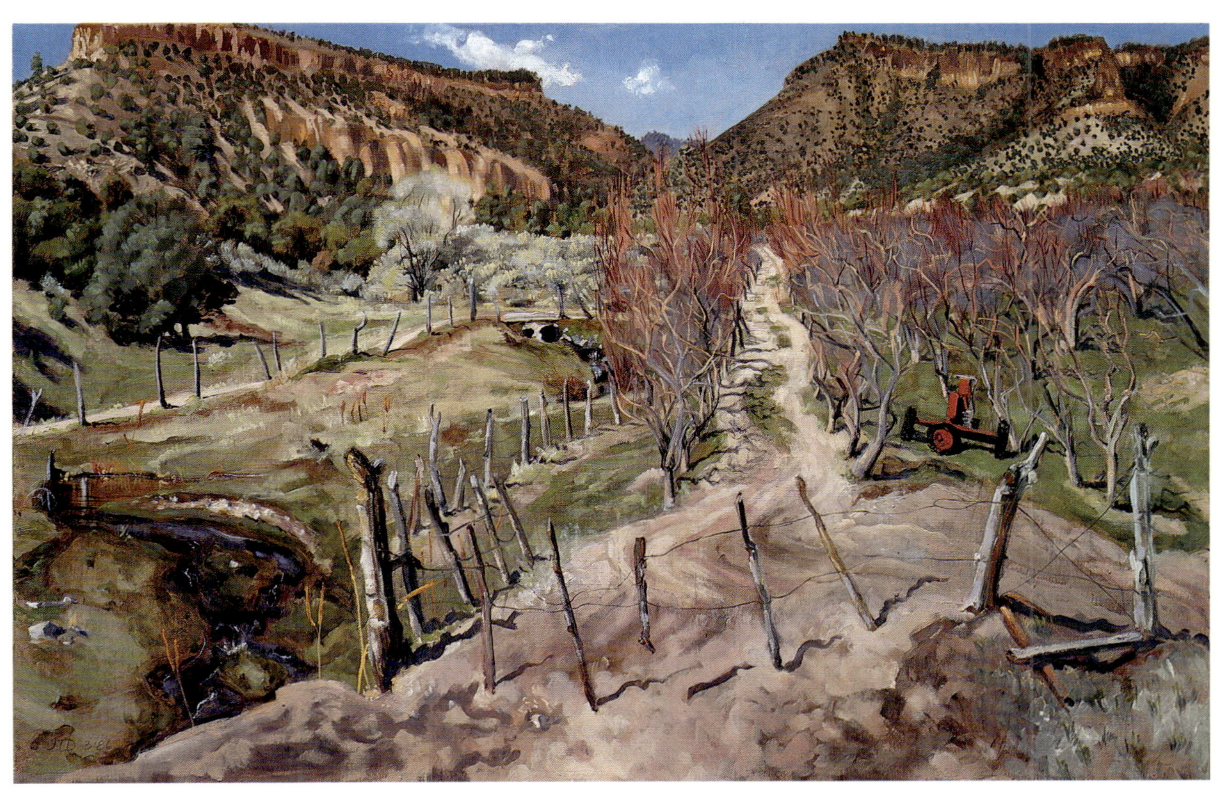

8   *Chatfield Reservoir, Chamisa and Snow,* January, 1986.
Oil on linen, 16 × 32 in.
Initialed lower right.

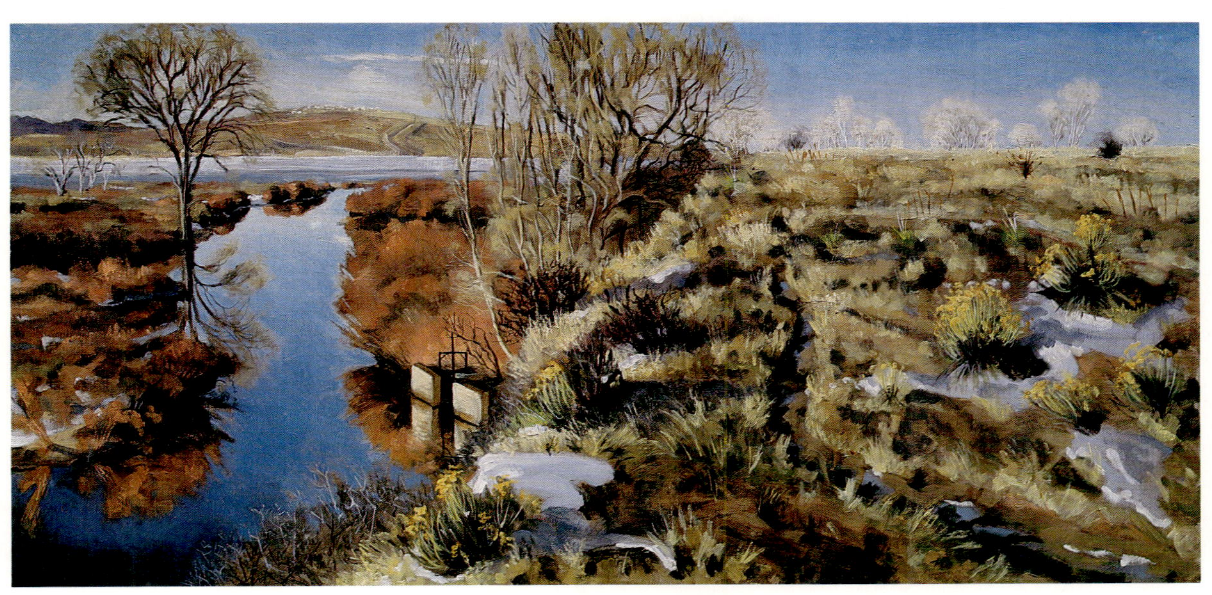

9   *Taos at Noon from the Gorge*, August 12, 1985.
Oil on panel, 7¾ × 14 in.
Initialed lower left.

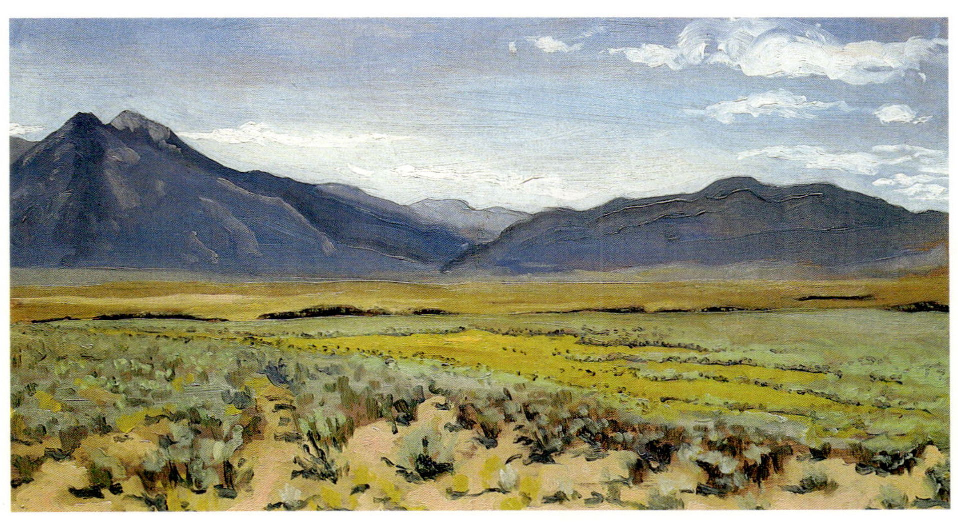

10   *Red Hills, Abiquiu,* August 11, 1985.
Oil on panel, 11¾ × 23¾ in.
Initialed lower right.

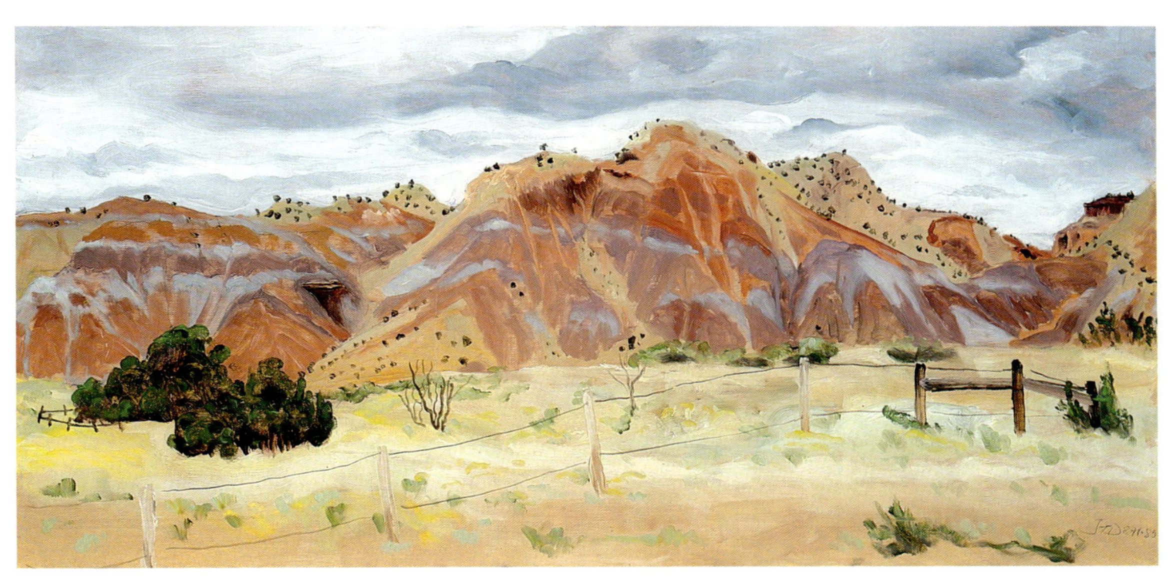

11   *Chimayo Farms along Route 76*, February, 1986.
Oil on linen, 22 × 28 in.
Initialed lower left.

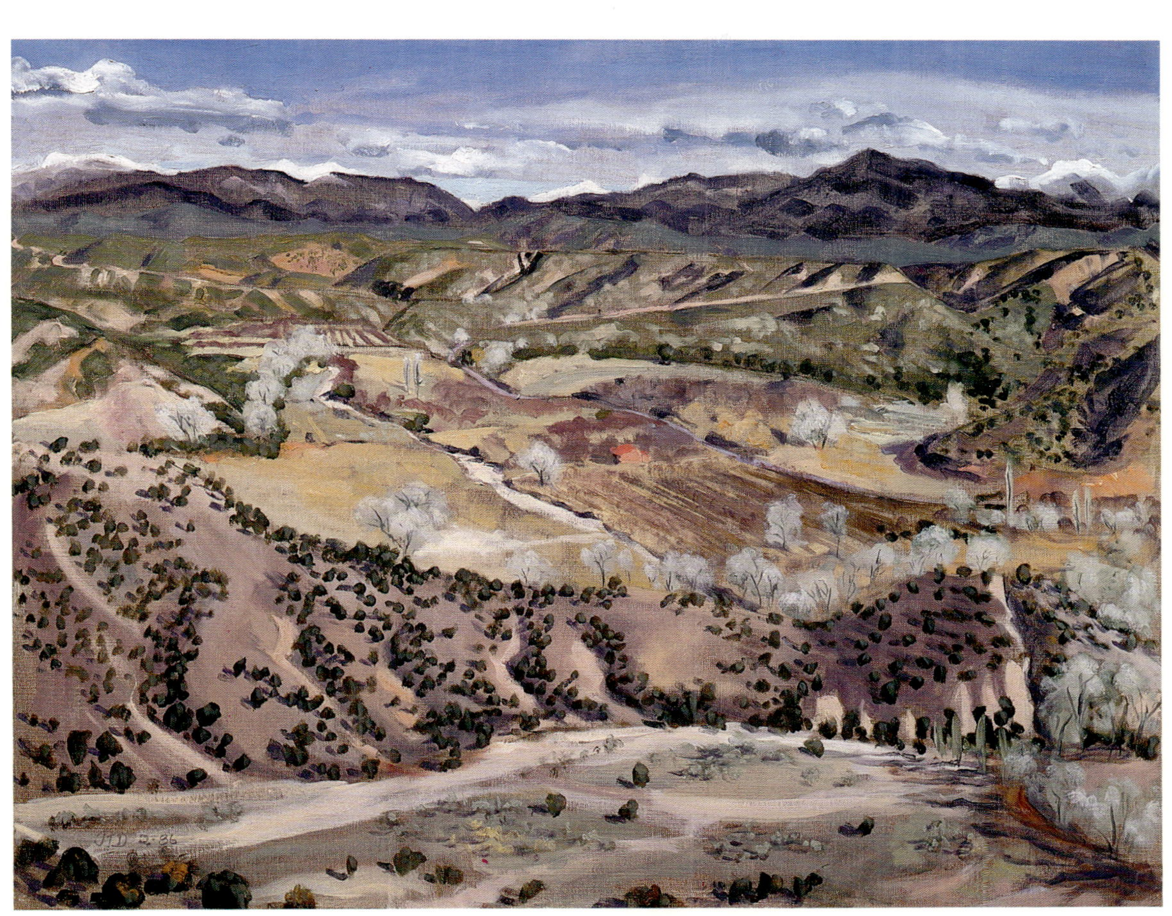

12   *Red Hills and Ruth's Rock*, January, 1986.
Oil on linen, 28 × 22 in.
Initialed lower right.

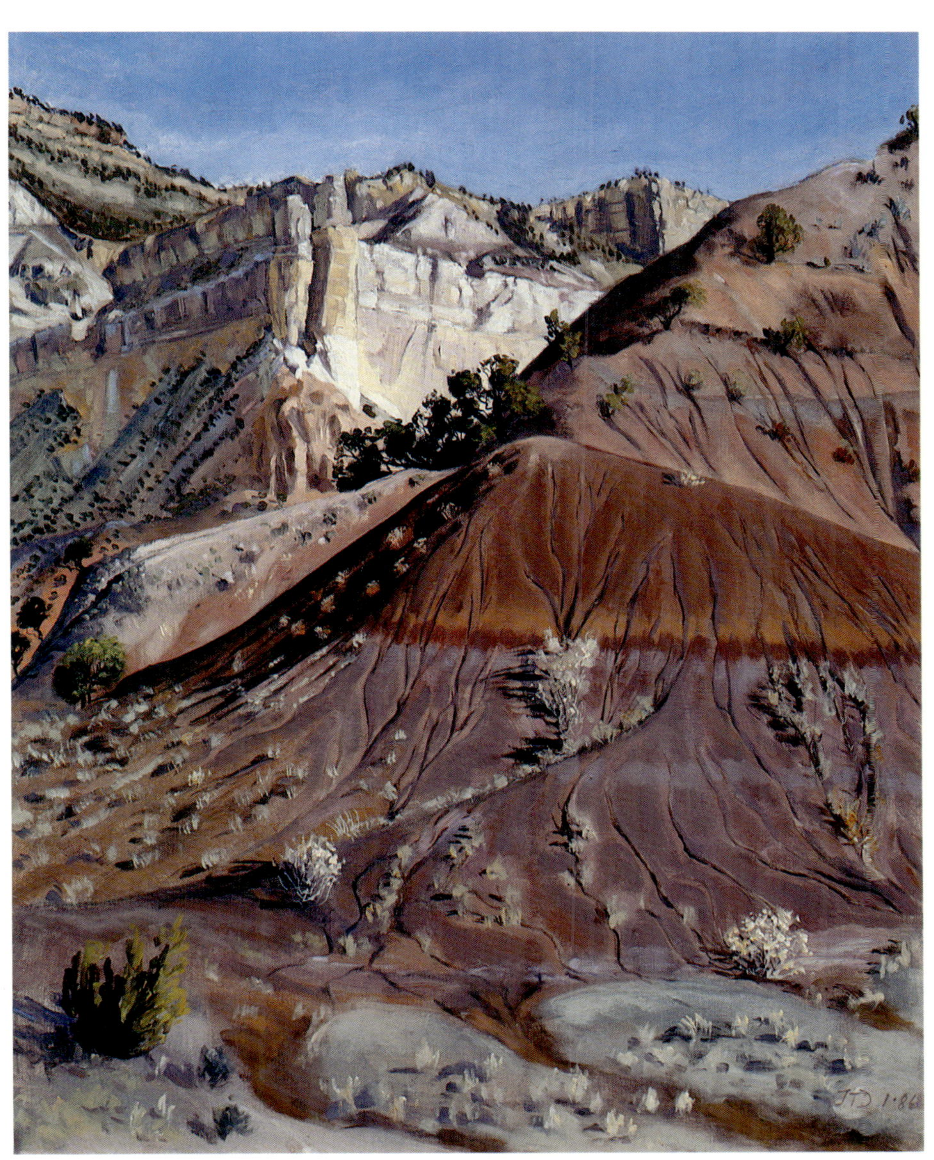

13   *Orchards at Velarde, New Mexico*, February, 1986.
Oil on masonite, 12 × 12 in.
Initialed lower left.

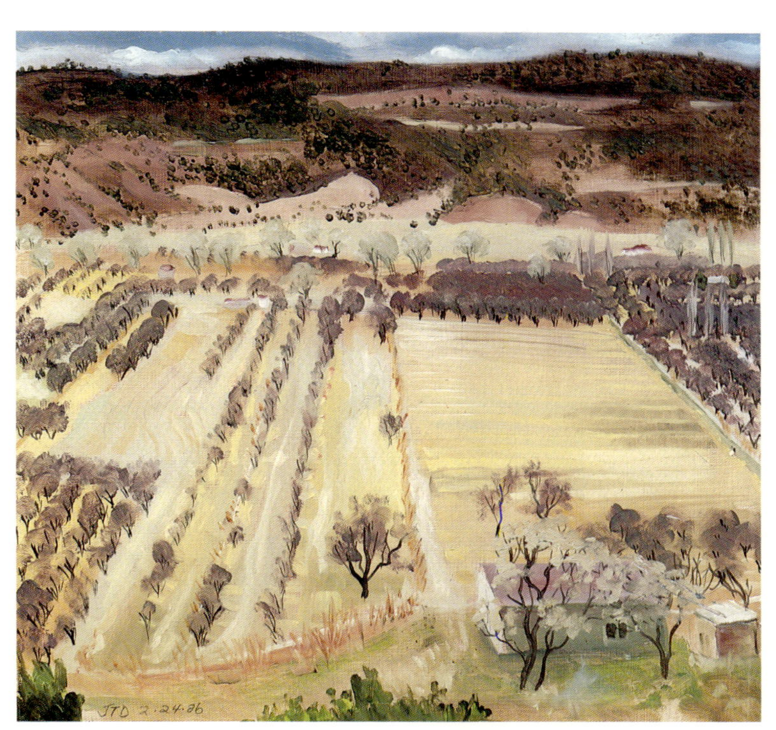

JTD 2·24·86

14   *Tin Roofs, Chimayo*, February, 1986.
Oil on masonite, 16 × 12 in.
Initialed lower left.

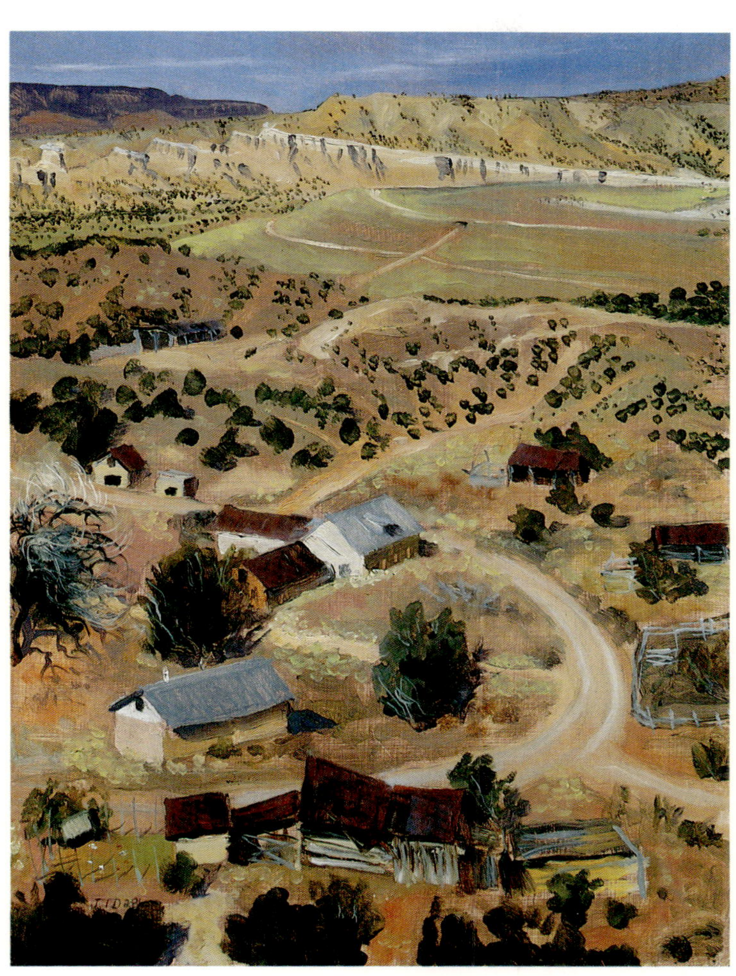

15   *Approaching Abiquiu*, August 11, 1985.
Oil on panel, 7¾ × 19¼ in.
Initialed lower left.

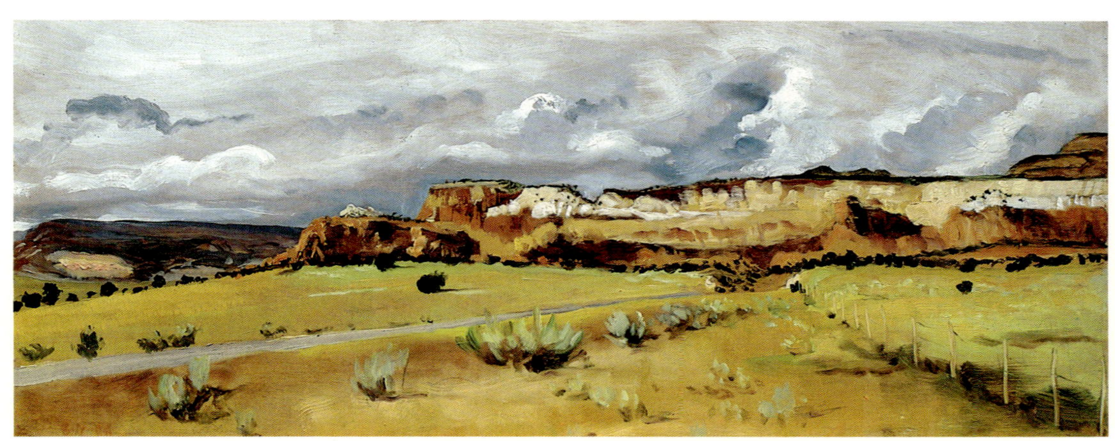

16   *Ice Fishing Huts at Chatfield*, January, 1985.
      Oil on board, 8 × 24 in.
      Initialed on reverse.

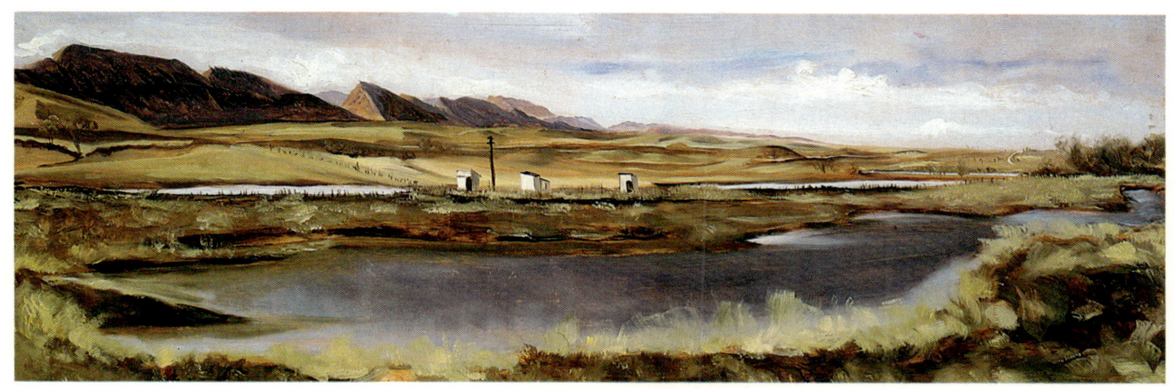

17   *Melting Pond Ice at Abiquiu*, January 10, 1986.
Oil on panel, 16 × 12 in.
Initialed lower right.

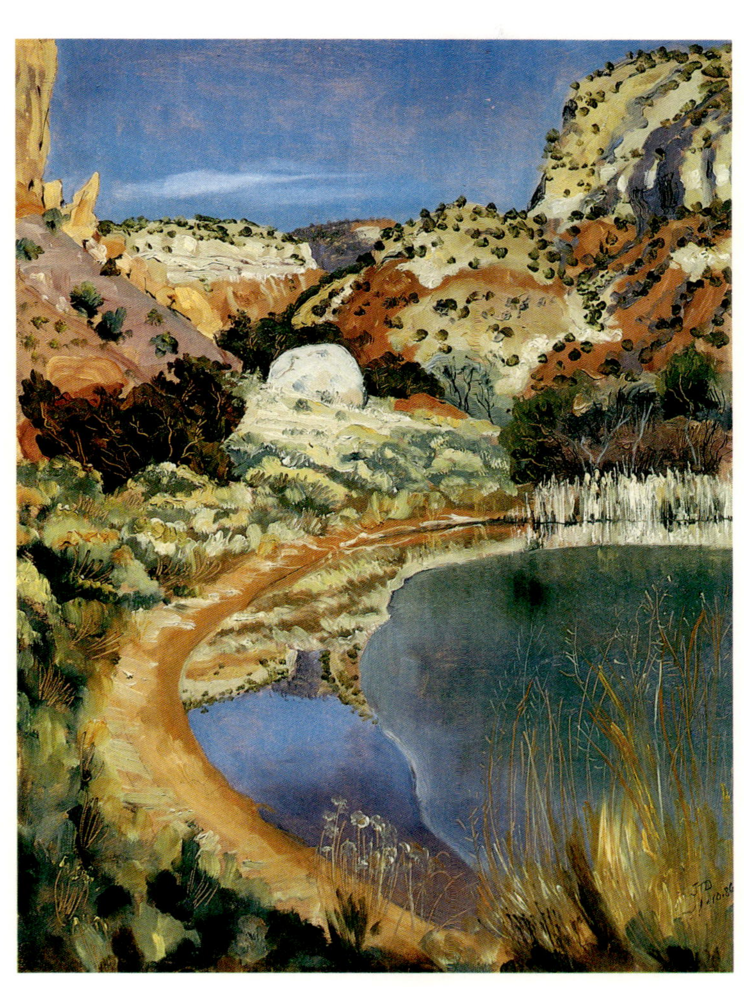

18   *Morning, Painted Desert at Abiquiu*, January, 1986.
Oil on panel, 12 × 8 in.
Initialed lower right.

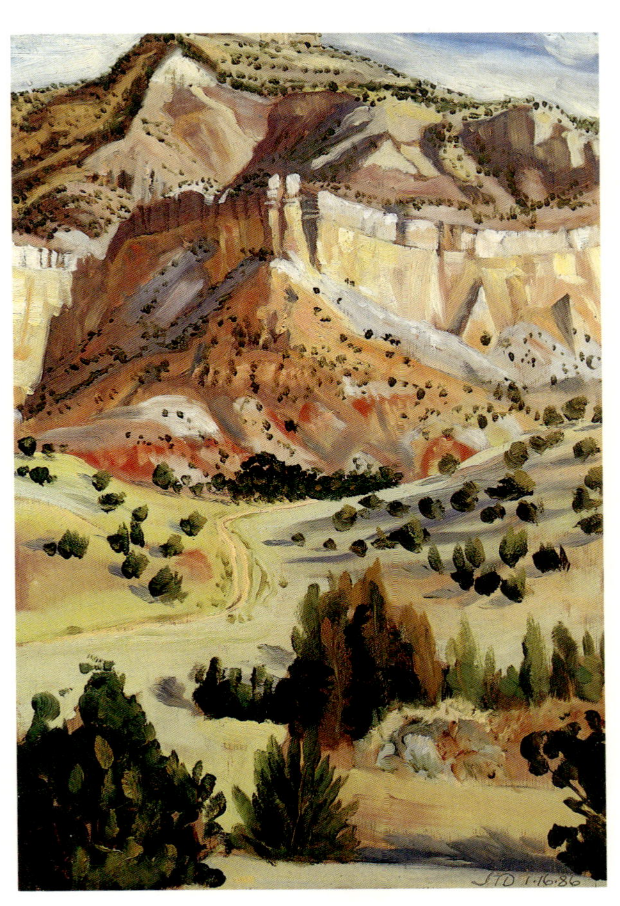

19   *Off Route 16 near Peña Blanca*, March 17, 1986.
Oil on panel, 5½ × 11½ in.
Initialed lower left.

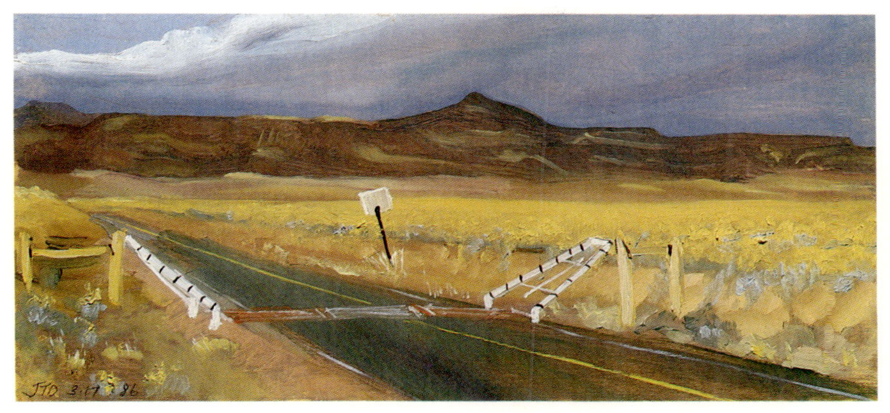

20   *Road to La Cañada Ruin*, March 21, 1986.
Oil on linen, 16 x 20 in.
Initialed lower left.

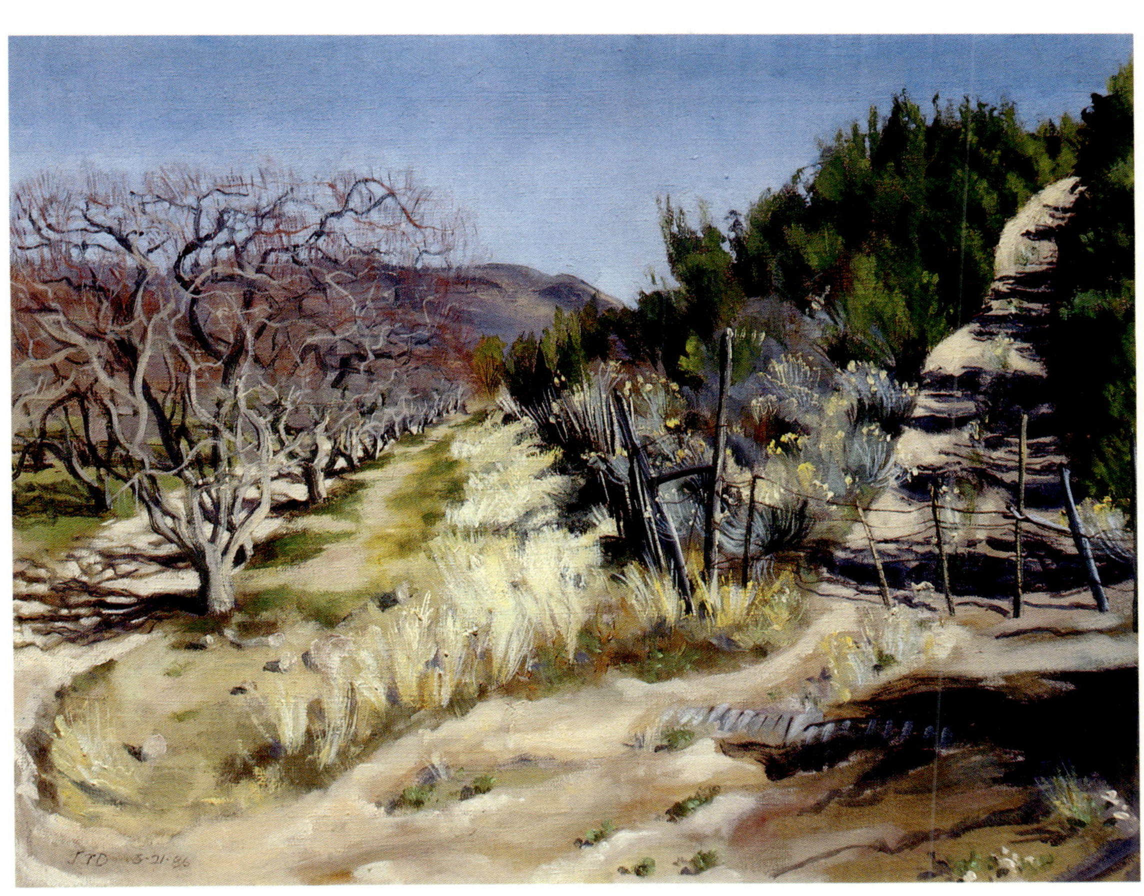

JOELLYN DUESBERRY

Born: June 30, 1944, Richmond, Virginia

EDUCATION:

Mary Washington College of the University of Virginia
Smith College, Massachusetts
Dartmouth College, New Hampshire
New York University, Institute of Fine Arts
Art Students League, New York
National Academy of Design, New York
New York Academy

EXHIBITED:

1968 Execution of wall murals and catalogue illustrations for *Mastercraftsmen
of Ancient Peru*, Guggenheim Museum, New York
1969 Execution of illustrations and maps for the exhibition catalogue, *Before
Cortes*, Metropolitan Museum of Art, New York
1979 and 1980 Group Exhibitions, Tatistcheff Gallery, New York
1982 and 1985 Solo Exhibition, Tatistcheff Gallery, New York
1982 *Hudson River Update*, The Gallery at Hastings-on-Hudson, New York
1982 *Contemporary Realism*, The Museum Gallery, New York
1983 The Du Pont Gallery, Mary Washington College of the University of Virginia
1984 Solo Exhibition, Reynolds–Minor Gallery, Richmond, Virginia
1986 Solo Exhibition, Gerald Peters Gallery, Santa Fe, New Mexico

CORPORATE COLLECTIONS:

Chemical Bank, New York
General Electric, Fairfield, Connecticut
HBO, Atlanta
Southeast Banking Corporation, Miami
Security Pacific Bank, Los Angeles
R. J. Reynolds, Winston-Salem
The St. Paul Companies, Minnesota
AT&T, New York
Pittsburgh Plate Glass Industries
March & McClennan, New York
Goldman Sachs, New York
Tupperware, Kissamee, Florida
U.S. Insurance Group, Morristown, New Jersey

AWARDS:

1966–67 Woodrow Wilson Fellowship
1985–86 National Endowment for the Arts Grant

PUBLICATIONS:

1971 *The Art Gallery Magazine*, April
1982 *Art/World*, February
1982 *The New York Times*, Sunday, February 7
1983 *The New York Times*, Sunday, November 13
1984 *American Artist*, February
1984 *Richmond News Leader* and *Richmond Times-Dispatch*, November 17 and 18
1984 *Art News*, March
1985 *Arts Magazine*, October